Magnolia House

Anonymous

ISBN: 1726318974
ISBN-13: 978-1726318976

CONTENTS

FORWARD

The division of North and South Korea has left a bitter mark of conflict and sorrow on the peninsula for the past 70 years. The 38 parallel that was drawn in my country was more than just a political, ideological divide; it was a separation of loved ones and an end to the 5000 years of history that a unified Korea once built together.

Ever since, North Korea has become the 21st century's greatest slaughterhouse in the minds of the public. North Koreans are often simplified as mere objects of subjugation and oppression. Sentiments of pity and anger for them overshadow true empathy and understanding.

Anonymous

While testimonies of North Korean refugees have
provided valuable insight into the mysterious shroud
of North Korea, their stories are too often degraded in
a political tool to criticize the Kim regime. The key
component in any story—a sense of connection—
lacks between the refugees and the rest of the world.

By translating their genuine voices in this book, I aim
not to provoke but to share. The voices of refugees
have more to offer than fear and defeatism; in the
essence of their stories exists a message of hope and
resilience, and they ought to be shared, loud and clear.

Haze Lee

Original copies of the memoirs and pictures were taken from the website "Rest for Refugees" (http://toxjals.com/). All profit made from the publication of Magnolia House will be donated to the Korea Hana Foundation, a non-profit public organization that supports North Korean refugees' resettlement in South Korea.

落葉歸根

낙엽귀근

"A leaf falls to return to its roots"

For my separated people.

Magnolia House

THE TUMEN

#1

Four days passed since your disappearance. The sky was jet black. Angry men stormed into our house without a knock, their eyes glinting with malice. Rooms that I had once kept spotlessly clean became filthy with their muddy footprints. The men carried shackles and guns, even an AK-47. They violently handcuffed your dad and me and threw us into a cargo truck like a sack of potatoes. As you know, a runaway's crimes are always paid for, one way or another. Being the parents of a runaway, we were locked in a prison cell where the smell of urine and waste permeated the air. It was only after three months of intense interrogation that we were allowed to leave. My son, o' my dear son, will your poor mother ever get to see you again?

By the time my mother's letter reached me, it was crumpled and folded so many times her handwriting was hard to read. The letter was kept hidden as it went through many hands before it found mine. It was only after three years that sheer luck brought it to me. The person who delivered the letter did not know whether my parents were alive or not. It was time's plague when no legged creatures could stand proud.

#2

Our family's loyalty to the communist party was well known. Those who did not know of our family's arrest must have wondered why we disappeared. Rumors in the countryside spread like wildfire, but as days passed and difficulties continued, new gossip arose to console people and help them forget about their own sufferings. Soon enough, we were forgotten by the world— except for one person, that is.

"J" was my girlfriend. I couldn't tell her anything before I left. I disappeared without a single word because if the party asked her where I went, it would be better for her not to know. Its torture can make even the most silent of people talk. I went to meet J the night before I fled. I talked to her as if it was any other day. It was hard to imagine a life without her, but all I could do was laugh to hide my sadness. Behind my smile lurked a miserable shadow.

"See you tomorrow," I said to her.

It was a promise I could not keep. That tomorrow never came. I hoped that J would understand the meaning of "tomorrow" someday. At dawn the next day, I left for the border. J must have come to our house, knocking on our door. She must have then realized that we had disappeared into thin air. As J steadily understood that I had fled, we completed our incomplete farewells. Our premature parting progressed, slowly and silently.

#3

My bag was very light as I left everything behind— the photo album that captured glimpses of the past 20 years of my life, the diary that I used to write secretly at night when nobody was around, my Chosun Language Dictionary that I used every day and the small notes I left in its corners. I threw away my past self and the things I cherished. I shed my history like a lizard sheds its tail. The uncertain days that were to come did not promise me the chance of looking back on past memories. My desire to remember the past was an extravagance I could not afford.

If I died during my escape, my regrets of leaving so much behind would be meaningless. If I survived, I would be losing my only time machine to the past. I write these entries based on the memories that I tried so hard not to forget. I scrounge around to find the last few drops of water left in the dry well of my past memories.

#4

I had to go to Hweng Ryeong, a province that shares a border with China 80 kilometers away from home. Fleeing without travel documents in the obscure mists of dawn, felt like a blind man trying to hike up a mountain. I could have been stopped at a checkpoint or arrested by a security guard— nobody knew what would happen. Is there anything like the fear of knowing that you know absolutely nothing?

I heard that as more people tried to cross the border, four more checkpoints were created. What were the chances of passing them safely? I did not know. Even if I knew the numbers of those that passed and those that died, there were too many variables to take into account.

I was caught in the last checkpoint. A security guard with the eyes of a snake stripped me of the hopes of making it to the border. I had tried to blend into a group of people that had travel documents in the back of a truck. Being too natural must have seemed unnatural to him.

"But sir I need to get food for my family." I said.

"That is no excuse to try and pass without documents!" Snake Eyes screamed.

Luckily, Snake Eyes fell for my excuse and did not order an arrest immediately. They didn't put handcuffs or tied ropes around me. Instead, I was thrown into a cargo truck, headed back to the direction of my home. Snake Eyes ordered the driver to take me to the region's security center. The truck started its engine. As soon as the checkpoint was out of sight, I leapt from the truck when I had the chance. I landed on my knees, hitting a rock. Blood oozed and streamed down my knees. The pain was excruciating as it spread throughout the body like electric waves, making my heart twinge. I ripped my shirt and tied it around the cut the best I could and started out on the road. Ten minutes later, I hitchhiked on a bus that took me to Hweng Ryeong. I had passed the first obstacle.

#5

When I got to the broker's house, he quickly hid me in a small room connected to the backyard. The housekeeper prepared fish for dinner. The fish was alive as it flapped around for its life. Did instinct make the fish believe that desperate flapping would get it back to the river? Sharpening a knife on a rock, I examined the fish and its eye. It gasped and gulped for air as a human would underwater. Humans underwater and fish outside of water throw a fit because of the hostility of the environment and the pain it brings. With that thought, the air suddenly felt thin, and I needed to breathe, breathe a little more. I turned around so that the fish didn't have to see the knife. Did it know its imminent death? Did it realize that a knife was being prepared to cut open its intestines and chop off its head? Did it understand that this knife would make an orbit around its body, separating its flesh and bones as its life ends on a cutting board? How did one understand death in the moment of death— or is it just that this creature did not understand its fate due to the torturous pain it felt at the moment?

The possibility of my fate being the same as the fish's

made me depressed. It was as if a rope was being slowly tied around my throat, tightening and making infinite knots. I wanted to save the fish, but my hunger got the better of me, and I could not keep it alive .

That night, I realized that it was the same thing for the guards that were trying to arrest me. If I got punished, they would live. If I lived, they would be punished. Those bastards that caught me would be able to return to their wives, smiling like a deer with pork they bought fresh from the market. I understood the bastards that were trying to catch me because to the fish, the bastard was me. I understood the fish and I understood the bastards. I even understood Snake Eyes.

#6

According to the law, those that let people without travel documents stay in their homes pay heavy consequences when caught. Because I was in a region so close to the border, suspicions ran high as anybody could be a South Korean spy or a runaway. Guards at times would suddenly search the house to arrest such "outlaws".

The border between North Korea and China may seem like a solid fence, but it often laps due to those that cross the river. The deals made between unpaid soldiers and brokers are what decide whether or not you can cross the border.

Every nerve in my body was alive and I couldn't go to sleep. That night, I learned that in the trenches, there was no such thing as atheists— the fear of being arrested made me believe in God. As the bright moonlight peaked in through a small window, I kneeled in the dark corners of the room, muttering a prayer.

"God, if there was a reason I was born and if I serve any purpose in this world, please let me cross the river safely."

My prayers were abruptly interrupted by the guard's

pounding on the door and the dogs wildly barking. Abruptly, I ran out of the room through the back door and hid myself in a pig pen. Inside the pen, the pig was taking a nap after a big meal, full and content. The pig lived in comfort and laziness while I shivered in fear and anxiety. The famous saying that it is better to be a sad human than a happy pig felt like nonsense. Would people be able to utter such nonsense in the face of death? I was jealous of the pig, sleeping without a worry in the world. But I knew that this pig would never escape the pen. Although it was lying in comfort and I was crouching in fear, I was the superior being because at least I had the courage to escape my country which was in a way a pen that restricted and raised us like livestock. I was on an adventure to escape the system that forcefully limited my potential and branded my identity on me. Even if I was arrested, I was ready to run away as long as there was a pint of breath left in my body.

#7

Did I see a resemblance between the pig that did not know the world outside the pen and my people that didn't know what awaited them outside their country?

It was a September afternoon three years ago. The autumn sun was warm and the sky spread out endlessly. My father, who imported livestock feed from China for a living, sneaked in some books over the border, secretly hiding them in the bags of feed. Most of the time when passing customs, the guards search the cargo with long sticks, feeling around the insides of the bags to see that no "objects of capitalism" are brought along. Seeing that my father returned safely, they did not catch him and his books. That night, my father handed me the books under the blankets. I held the books tightly— they had smooth, white pages. Although he did not say anything, his eyes were telling me not to get caught with these books.

One of the books taught me about philosophy. Under the 3W battery flashlight and the safety of my blanket,

I spent all night reading that book. I hungrily devoured the book that showed me a world so entirely different from the world I've known so far. This new world I was introduced to was so different from the things that the news spokesman scorned of every night on TV— the law of the jungle, the increasing disparity between the rich and poor, and the rotten ideals of capitalism— in the book, new ideas and dynamics existed and collided. Such ideas were unheard of in North Korea. In the book, the ultimate truth was questioned and pursued as everyone debated on a common ground.

One of the most impactful philosophers was Plato. In the book, Plato talked about prisoners that were born in a cave who believed that the shadows of their figures were real. One of the prisoners later escaped from the cave and in the outside world although he felt pain, shock, and embarrassment, he also got to feel the sun, the evergreen forest, and the wind.

I felt that the loyal people of my country, staring at the image of Kim Jong Il on TV with their empty, soulless eyes were like the prisoners. It was a country where the growling stomachs of the people were ignored while the only newspaper in the nation, "Labor News", continued to praise our "beautiful country". My country was a cave.

After the death of Kim Il Sung, North Korea became a muted chaotic mess. There were no visible massacres and nobody heard thunderous sounds of bombs. Instead, little by little, the floors of the rice jar became visible day by day and one by one, people started to die. One left his hometown in search for food and died in the streets because of hypothermia. Another one ate things that could not be digested and died rubbing his stomach in pain. The threats of starvation found my family as well and my father's thin elbows and my mother's tender back weakly swayed by the wind of death. Questioning what to eat and resisting hunger became the number one priority.

I wanted to escape from this cave. The book stuck to me like a parasite in my brain, leading me and demanding me to go to a new world. I was ready to escape the pen of totalitarianism to a land of liberty and democracy.

#8

The chilliness of the northern winds that night may have been what had stopped the guards from checking the smelly pig pen. When they left at a little over 1 a.m., my frozen body quietly crept out of the pen towards the Tumen River with the broker as my guide. The bright light of the moon scrutinized my face. The broker told me that it was the perfect night to cross the river. It was April 25th, a national holiday when soldiers drank and their guard was down. The broker also pointed out that the soldiers wouldn't imagine that there would be a person insane enough to try crossing the river in such a bright night. The part of the Tumen we were trying to cross was 100 meters wide. The water was more than 6 feet deep. It was rapid and the floors were slippery.

"Are you sure you won't regret it?", asked the broker.

What is the meaning of "regret"? I really did not understand. If I didn't cross the river, would anything happen to me that is better than crossing the river? How would I know the answer without even attempting to cross? I mockingly laughed at the emptiness of the word "regret". Whether I stayed or crossed, my future would be unclear. I couldn't be in two places simultaneously. I did not know what people I would meet and where I would go the next day, whether it was China or North Korea. It was something you just couldn't compare.

#9

The river bank was eerily tall like a graveyard in the night of the moon. How many people would have tried to climb this bank? The scene reminded me of a poem written by Ki Cheon Cho.

Behind are prison and death
In front is nameless danger
Protecting the corner like a cat

In the borders of China and North Korea, life and death collided. The northern cold turned the air into a sharp knife. The blood that ran in the veins of my 20 year old self was instantly frozen. The cold twisted my flesh and reached my bones, but the urge to get over the wall and face what fate had prepared for me and the curiosity of what the next ten minutes would bring me overcame the cold. There were many possibilities— my body being ripped by a soldier's gun and knife, getting struck by a bullet that would shatter my skull, or by luck, crossing the river safely— but I did not know what would happen. Such helplessness amplified my fear.

As I climbed the wall, flat on the stomach, the sounds of the river rapids grew fiercer. 50 meters ahead of me, I saw the grand Tumen river, shining white. I crawled along the gravel and sand until I reached the river. Although the perfectly round moon illuminated everything as the sun would, I could not see anything. I carefully crept along the slanted dike, my heart pounding recklessly. I slithered like a snake.

"Clink, clink"

My body got entangled with ropes tied to an empty can. These were traps made by soldiers to catch runaways. The sound made my mind go blank.

The broker sharply whispered, "Run!".

"Halt!"

The soldiers that abruptly woke up ran after me, blowing whistles and screaming. When I glanced back, I saw the soldier's hollow cheekbones and the moonlight glinting on it, making him look like a skeleton.

All the hair on my body stood. I jumped into the water. I swam. My arms and legs fought the water ferociously. I dove. I could not breath. I needed to breathe so bad, but would you risk a gulp of air for your life? Gunshots were followed by gunshots. The night was fierce and the sky ripped apart as it rumbled like thunder. Whether the sound was gunshots or my heartbeat, I did not know.

The waters of the Tumen are usually frigid in April. But in the April of 2007, when I was crossing the river at dawn, hearing the sounds of screaming bullets coming after me, I was a little creature lost between the realms of life and death, senseless to the numbing cold.

#10

What would have taken half a day in a straight line distance to my apartment in Seoul took an year for me to reach. Although it is a land where birds are free to fly and migrate, it is still a cave to oppressed people. A year after I received the letter from my mother, I was finally reunited with my parents.

It has been 10 years since I've started my new life in South Korea. At times I remember the broker's question whether I will regret leaving home or not. I remember with a tired heart the sleepless nights the philosophy book had brought. I still remember the night I crossed the river with fear for my life. I see the troubles of the people who continue to live in that land, barely making it. I feel the fear of the people who are caught by guards and soldiers, trying to cross the border. I can imagine the pupils of the countless mothers and children, young girls and boys whose body lay under the Tumen. If we can say that all people have their own separate little worlds, how many universes and worlds have ceased to exist in that river?

I would not be able to change the fixed relations of the North and South, but I can still smile warmly and say another kind word to make this world a better place. It is for such modest dreams that I faced dangerous times and overcame helplessness to march forward, on and on.

The Tumen River

STARLIGHTS OF MY HOMELAND

I look up at my stars, twinkling in the night sky. My stars can be seen from the backyard of the Northern home I was born and raised in. My stars can be seen from the opposite side of the peninsula where I stand, somewhere down, deep in the South. My stars are eternal; they do not change; but alas, I can no longer look at them from the backyard of my homeland. O my homeland, how I miss your mountains and rivers. When, o when will you take me to the loving arms of my parents and brothers. We have fled from you but we cannot forget you. O my homeland, I want to tell you that our wish is unification, the word we desperately cry for with the world on our side. The 38 parallel that divides us shall melt by the heat of the sun and its molten iron will harden to become a bridge. From then on, the winds will take us to you, where we will mourn for the fallen bodies of our parents that lie deep down in you. O homeland, my dear homeland, we await for the day of unification when we will be reunited once again.

LIMP

I was out in Cheongjin station on my way to my uncle's. A man came up to me and asked for some food. His face was as pale as chalk and it was obvious that he had not eaten for days. His bones were visible and he had the legs of a skeleton. The man carried a baby boy on his back and was holding hands with another child. I presumed the two were brothers, the one on the back younger and the other older. I wished I had something to give them, but I had no food.

A soldier standing nearby ransacked his backpack and took out a piece of bread to give to the father. The father immediately split the bread into two and gave one to each of the boys, but when he tried to slip the bread into the baby boy's hands, the child wasn't able to hold on to it. The bread slipped and gently fell on the ground. At that moment, something felt instinctively wrong. The father abruptly reached out for his boy but it was too late. The baby boy's arms were limp as his final breath left his body. Unaware of what happened, the other brother crouched down and hungrily devoured the bread that his dead brother had let go.

Imagine the agony of a father who couldn't feed his own son, whose stomach was no bigger than a man's fists. The father's body went limp.

SPRING SHALL COME

My heart flutters at the thought of spring. I hope spring has arrived in your heart as well. When spring comes, even the frozen Han and Tumen River melt, their bodies dancing. Ironic it is, considering that the 38 parallel of our hearts remain frozen.

As the seasons change and spring comes, I think of our homeland more often. At least I can visit there in my wildest dreams to run in the fields that I played in back when we were children. I wonder if I will ever get to visit those fields again.

I wish a tsunami can come, a tsunami big enough to

topple down the parallel. Can nature grant my wish, or am I wishing for too much? I shall march from the South and you from the North, and we shall march until our spring comes, not only to our seasons but also to our hearts. Until that day comes, I will work and pray. When spring ends, summer will come, followed by autumn and winter. Time goes and the sun changes, but until true spring comes to the 38 parallel, we shall wait. No matter how many times the magnolias bloom and wither, even if we wither ourselves and become mere spirits, we shall wait. And spring shall come.

A DARK SUN

"Kyung Ho, Jun Young came. Wake up!" Mother cried out from the kitchen, making breakfast.

"You told me not to be late, Kyung Ho. How come you're not up yet?" Jun Young said, peeking through the door. The door was open to let the smoke out from all the cooking. I was wrapped in a blanket like a *danmuji* in a *kimbap*. I could barely open my eyes.

"Huh, you're already here Jun Young? Just wait a bit. I'll be there in a sec." I said.

I glanced at the clock. It was five in the morning. How in the world that boy woke up so early, I did not know. Jun Young lived near a military office ten minutes away from my house. He seemed nervous for the first day of work. He was seventeen that year.

Jun Young was the head of his family and had a younger sister to look after. He was still young— it had only been a year since he graduated middle-high school— but after his father died in the railroad tracks when he was five and his mother became bedridden due to a heart disease, Jun Young had to learn how to be mature very early for his age.

But enough about Jun Young— this is a story about his mother.

It was about ten years ago when poverty hit the country and people had to live on grass roots and tree bark. To survive from the war against hunger and save her two young children, Ms.Kim started to sell blood sausages in the marketplace. Every morning she would buy pig intestines from the butcher and spend the night making sausages. At night Jun Young and Mi Young would wake up from the smell of sausages and sit next to her, drooling at the thought of them. It broke Ms.Kim's heart that she could not give them anything but the water that came out of the sausages. With the money made from the sausages they themselves could not eat, Ms.Kim fed the family of three.

One day in the streets as Ms.Kim took out a sausage from the steam pot, a handsome gentleman wearing fancy clothes and black sunglasses walked up to her and asked for a piece of sausage. Ms.Kim thought it was good luck that the first customer of the day was a rich man and she happily flowered him with compliments and smiles.

"Have any liquor?"

Grabbing a chair, the gentleman sat down.

Although everybody sold liquor in the marketplace, they had to keep it hidden in fear of getting caught by the market security guards or the anti-capitalism group members. Such people would jump on vendors if they saw liquor out on the streets. It was only after a customer asked for a cup that the vendors would quietly sneak one out of their stands.

Ms.Kim looked left and right and quickly snatched out a bottle that was hidden under a cloth. She filled a glass full of it and pleasantly gave it to the gentleman.

"Is work hard in the marketplace these days? How many mouth do you have to feed?" the gentleman asked.

"I was widowed three years ago. I come here every day to feed my two children." she answered honestly.

"I am deeply sorry for your loss... May I ask how it happened?" he murmured.

"He was working in the railways when an onsetter accidentally backed a locomotive, trying to connect a hose. The machine crushed his body."

The gentleman nodded his head in sympathy but a part of his eyes looked strange as it steadily scanned Ms.Kim's body. Ms. Kim used to dance from a young age and even after having two children, she had the body of a dancer. Her face was a pretty one, and she looked young for her age. As the liquor worked on the gentleman, his eyes began to glint in desire under his black sunglasses.

They talked for twenty minutes as he emptied the bottle and the plate. Once he was done, the gentleman slowly got up and brought out a bill of 500 won. The sausage was 100 won and the booze was 50 won, but the gentleman being her first customer of the day, she did not have 350 won to give for change. Ms.Kim was flustered and did not know what to do as she held onto the 500 won bill.

"Don't worry about it," the gentleman said. Ms.Kim's eyes became big. "I'll come often from now on. You can give me change next time." smiling, he waved and left.

The women selling blood sausages next to Ms. Kim looked at her with half jealousy and half envy, telling her how lucky she was and how nice it must be to be pretty. Some even warned her to be careful of such men, but nothing could waver Ms.Kim's spirits. She was happy for the rest of the day and she bought brand new notebooks for Jun Young and Mi Young with the money, something she could rarely do.

Married at the age of 23 and having lost a husband at 29, Ms.Kim had lived solely for her children for the past three years. Her mother back home wanted her to come back home to the countryside and get remarried, but Ms.Kim was faithful and loyal, refusing to leave the house that her dead husband had left for her. Many came to her with pictures of suitors asking for her hand but she would reject them, telling them she had no intentions of meeting another man.

But Ms.Kim was only 30 years old, a ripe age when a person needed a relationship. And as time passed and her wounds healed, loneliness and solitude crept into her as her heartaches slowly subsided. She felt resentful of her husband who had left her at such an early age with young children to look after, and she couldn't help but yearn for stability and reliability. The guilt, however, that she felt for her dead husband and two children prevented her from falling into such desires.

A few days later, the gentleman came back around the time he visited last time. The woman sitting next to Ms.Kim noticed the gentleman walking towards her.

"Look, dear, it's that man again." she said.

Ms.Kim was surprised to see him. The gentleman ignored all other stands and came straight up to Ms.Kim.

"How are you? I'd like some booze and a plate of sausages. I meant to come sooner but I've been busy because of work in the company these days. How's Jun Young?"

The two talked like old friends. Ms.Kim's heart fluttered at the thought that he went to a "company" (could it be an international trading company? she wondered) and appreciated him for remembering Jun Young's name. She brought out the 350 won she always kept just in case the gentleman returned, but the man did not accept it. Instead he gulped down the liquor and ate the blood sausages.

"I'm an employee in the *Inmin*'s *Cheolsong* Trading Company," he said, taking out his name card. "I live in Apartment 7 by the Aprok River. Perhaps you have heard of the place?"

Ms.Kim gulped. Heard of that place? Ms.Kim knew very well that only the wealthiest of the country lived in that apartment. The gentleman pompously explained that the marketplace was on his way to the company and that he came back from China yesterday from work. Ms.Kim was envious of the gentleman and thanked him many times for coming again. He waved his hand.

"The sausages here are exceptional Ms.Kim. You should work for a big restaurant and be the chef you are fit to be."

Ms.Kim's face grew read in embarrassment but the compliment pleased her. The gentleman handed her another 500 won and left without accepting change. From that day forth, the gentleman came every two days to eat sausages and drink, leaving a handsome amount of tip for Ms.Kim. At first she was uncomfortable with the amount of money that she was not used to, but she had no choice but to accept it for her family. A month passed and with the gentleman's frequent visits, the two became close.

"Ms.Kim would you like to work for a restaurant in

China that my company owns?"

"Why, I wouldn't be qualified." she said, surprised.

"You don't need to be a professional cook and the recipes are simple— stuff like *naengmyeon*. Besides, a lot of people in my company go there often and leave a large tip."

 Ms.Kim was tempted. She had neighbors who made a good living by sneaking in Chinese products over the border. If she could make a bit more money— but it would not do.

"I would like to go, but I have to look after my children." she said.

"I can have someone look after the kids and I'll pay for it. This is not an opportunity that comes too often Ms.Kim, and I'm simply trying to help you feed your kids. Choose wisely."

Born in the countryside of the Bocheon region, Ms.Kim had never traveled anywhere and the prospects of going to China thrilled her. She told him that she needed some time to think. The gentleman nodded, stood up and left.

A few days later, Ms.Kim came to our house. My mother and Ms.Kim were the only ones in the neighborhood that were born in Bocheon. They relied on each other like family in the best of times and the worst of times. When my father had a stroke a few years back, Ms.Kim nursed him back to health with my mother, the two of them spending long nights together. When Mr.Kim died because of an accident, my mother and Ms.Kim cried and hugged each other as if they were family.

That day Ms.Kim came, she told my mother everything about the gentleman and his offer. My mother opposed to the idea completely. She told Ms.Kim that she shouldn't trust an offer that was made by a stranger that wasn't from the government.

She also told her that Jun Young just started elementary school and that he needed his mother. Repeatedly, she warned her that in such times of famine, there were frauds that tricked and sold hungry people into human trafficking.

Ms.Kim bowed her head and seemed to hesitate but my mother could tell that her heart was already set on crossing the Aprok River. What Ms.Kim did not tell my mother that day was that the gentleman would at times visit her house late at night.

When Ms.Kim didn't appear in our doorsteps for more than two months, my mom told me to stop by the Kim household to see if everything is fine. When I got to Jun Young's house after school, the door was locked and the house looked abandoned. When I told my mother, she sighed and worried that Ms.Kim was tricked into a scam.

Months passed and my mother's worries turned into reality. Ms.Kim, who had left with the promise that she would come back with some money after a few months, did not return for six months, and then a year.

The next summer, 14 months since Ms.Kim had left, Jun Young's grandmother came to our house with Jun Young. She gasped for breath as she hurried into our house.

"She's back! My daughter!" she cried out.

"Where is she now? When did she come?" my mother asked, surprised.

"Yesterday a guard came and told me that she was captured by a Chinese police officer! She's in the county's jail right now for Christ's sake!" she sobbed.

Mother was shocked. Not a sound came out of her mouth. She quickly grabbed food from the house and ran over to the county jail in *Gang Gu Dong*. In North Korea, every county has a jail where those who cross the river illegally or travel without the right documents, tramps, and "anti-socialists" are kept. Most of them are people from the lowest classes of society awaiting their fate in jail before an interrogation with a judicial authority.

Mother told our neighbors to call father's friend who worked in the Bureau of Security to talk about Ms.Kim. When my mother, Jun Young, and his grandmother got there, the soldier in the front gate made some calls. Once he knew who my father was friends with, he saluted and told them to go in. Visiting someone outside of family is normally difficult but thanks to the phone call from the Bureau of Security, my mother was let in. They were let into the visiting room.

Few minutes later, a woman with a gaunt face that looked like wheat dried up in the summer heat came in. Once she saw them, she gasped and ran up to them. The four embraced and cried together. Ms.Kim went down on her knees and grabbed the hem of my mother's pants.

"I should have listened to you. I don't deserve to live." she sobbed.

The three were angry at Ms.Kim but their sadness was greater. With the help of my father's friend, Ms.Kim was able to get out after receiving only a month of labor camp. The day she got out, my mother and Ms.Kim cried once again as she thanked and apologized again and again. That night, she told us the full story.

As the gentleman visited more often, Ms.Kim spent more time trying to sell more sausages. One day she had sold most of her sausages by nine and was about to head back home when the gentleman appeared.

"I stayed in the company for way too long today. I'm really lucky to find you at such a late hour. Say, can I have a drink at your place?"

Ms.Kim wanted to decline because the hour was too late, but she didn't want to offend him after all the money he gave her. When they got to the house, the children were already asleep and the heat and smell from cooking sausages were still there. The room felt stuffy.

"We need to get you a new apartment for the kids. I'll help you when the time comes."

The gentleman said, looking around the room. He took off his overcoat and sat down.

"Thank you for being so kind. I'm really sorry but there's not much sausages left. There is some liquor though."

"That's fine. All I need is some booze." he said. Ms.Kim spread out all she had and the gentleman drank.

"Drink with me— work's over for today. Be my drinking companion." he smiled.

"Oh no, I don't really like drinking and I have to get up early in the morning to make sausages."

"How much do you make a day anyways, selling sausages?"

The man took out a big sum of money and offered it to her. Ms.Kim declined.

"It's very late and I have to go to the butcher's early in the morning. Please finish up soon."

The gentleman said he was slightly hurt and pushed the money into the corner of the room. He slowly got up. Ms.Kim was starting to feel sorry for asking him to leave so soon when the gentleman suddenly grabbed her from behind. Surprised, Ms.Kim almost yelled but the walls were thin and she was afraid of waking up the kids. Silently, she fought the hands groping for her.

The gentleman was a beast. He attacked her with a force she could not fight against. She used her fingernails and scratched his hands until it bled but it was no use. After a desperate fight, the man threw her on the ground and held down her arms with the force of his knees. He then attacked her breasts that were tense yet tender. As a last attempt, she spit on his face and then realized that there was nothing she could do anymore. As the man roughly panted and attacked her with his hands and mouth, she could feel her body unwillingly responding as it became hotter and wetter. She had lost the fidelity that she had tried so hard to keep for her dead husband. She gave away her body to the beast-like man as he went inside her, not even bothering to take his clothes off. Tears of disgust and guilt streamed down on Ms.Kim's face.

The next day, Miss Kim was consumed with the fact that she had failed to fight off the monster. She felt immense guilt she towards Mr.Kim and her children. Instead of going to the marketplace, she cried all day sitting by the Aprok River. The second day, she went to the graveyard where Mr.Kim was buried for atonement to cry and apologize to her dead husband.

The third day, around lunch, the gentleman visited her house again. Without waiting for an answer, he walked into the Kim household after a few knocks. The kids were at school and the neighbors were out of the house.

"Get out of my house!" she yelled.

The gentleman covered her mouth with one hand and grabbed her waist by the other. He carried her into the room and ripped off her clothes. Ms.Kim shrieked and resisted, but the deed was done again. Once the last drop of him was inside her body, he got up and sheepishly put on his clothes.

"Ms.Kim, I'm not taking advantage of you just because you're a widow. I have a wife and kids as well, but honestly, that day when I first saw you, I fell for you. And although I told myself over and over that I shouldn't, I couldn't help myself. Forgive me— I am truly sorry." he went down on his knees.

Ms.Kim remained silent and did not move. Then he slowly came and hugged her, helping her put on her pants. Innocent and kind Ms.Kim couldn't defy his hand. His words seemed sincere and she almost felt sympathy for him. Gradually, she let his hands on her body and sobbed in his shoulders.

Starting from that day, the gentleman did not visit the marketplace but went straight to Ms.Kim's house. He would come at night like a cat and disappear at dawn. Ms.Kim knew that they were having an affair but as she spent more time with him, she came to care for him and believe in everything he said.

His idea of her working in a restaurant in China was offered in the heights of their affair. She believed in him without much suspicion. Maybe it was because of her innocence, being raised deep in the countryside, or maybe it was her natural kindness, but Ms.Kim never in her wildest dreams suspected that the gentleman would do her any harm.

The gentleman told her that finishing the official paperwork and registering her as his company's employee would take too much time. He told her that it was better to simply cross the river back and forth, and she believed in him.

The night Ms.Kim sent Jun Young and Mi Young to their grandmother's house, the gentleman came to her house with another man. Telling her that the man would guide the way, the gentleman calmed her down. The three people crossed the Chin Sun bridge and reached the river dike. It was midnight when Ms.Kim saw two lights blink across the river. Two soldiers with guns approached her. Ms.Kim shuddered in fear. When they came near, however, they simply looked at her and went to talk to the man who led her there. After talking to the man, the soldiers soon disappeared.

The gentleman and the man took out a tractor tube that seemed to be prepared beforehand. They pumped air into it for ten minutes and when the tube got inflated enough, they put a cardboard on top of it.

"Get on the tube." the gentleman said.

Scared and not knowing what to do, she complied.

"Take your clothes off except for your underwear and give them to me."

Fear crept into her and Ms.Kim rolled up her clothes and handed them to him. She suddenly remembered the way the soldier looked at her with mocking eyes. She sensed something was wrong but it was too late. She was crossing the river.

There's no need to explain what happened next. It's obvious how things ended— Ms.Kim was sent to prison and later suffered from heart disease. She was one of many women in North Korea that were tricked into prostitution. Imagining Ms.Kim in her bed with her continuing nightmares, I looked at Jun Young's face that early morning. The weight he had to carry was heavy but his face was calm and confident. The sun had set on the Kim family, but it was ready to rise once more.

COUSIN

I used to have three cousins.

My youngest cousin was 10 years old. After he was abandoned by Aunt, my cousin would go out in the streets and plead for food to take care of my sick uncle.

One day, my cousin was in the streets as usual when a soldier gave him a piece of bread. My cousin, running back home to share the bread with his father, was hit by a car and died.

I had another cousin. She was three years old and the

only daughter of my aunt. My aunt had to go work in the market every day to feed and clothe her baby girl. The nursery of the government wouldn't take her baby in because my aunt didn't have a "real" job. One day, my cousin waited all day inside a locked room for my aunt to come back from the marketplace. Slowly sucking her slender fingers, she gently left this world.

My youngest uncle had a five year old son. When he came to our house, he would be the baby of the family, the center of attention, but my cousin couldn't leave the house because he had no shoes. He would pitifully whine to his mother how he wanted to go out and play. He cried and cried, asking her for shoes. My heart broke that I could not buy a single pair of sneakers for my cute little cousin, but my growling stomach ignored any form of pain that was not mine.

Even to this day, children in North Korea do not have the basic rights that most children have— the right to eat and run out to play.

Such memories make me guilty of my happiness as I convince myself every day that I have to live for the weak and poor. Some people say being happy is all there is to life. Maybe they're right. The world is such a happy place when I am unconscious of others and I only think of myself. But sometimes— and god knows why— I am overwhelmed with sadness and pain when I think of those that don't have nearly as much as me.

Are you truly there in the Heavens, God? What should I call this place in which I breathe? Should I be content of the fact that I am happy? Is there even a world where the kind and the honest live the life they deserve?

I try to calm my aching heart as I scribble these words down. I have shed many tears for the past six years I have been separated with my family, and someone else must be shedding the same tears this exact moment.

GRADUTATION FROM THE NORTH

The One Where Everything Began

It was February 24th, 2012 when I graduated from Yonsei University as a history major. That day, I was sitting with the graduating class, fiddling with my graduation cap. The only goal I had since the moment I entered college was to graduate from it. College may be a natural process for others but to me, it was a huge obstacle— how many hours had I worked for to get to this point? Tears rolled down my face as I remembered the past hardships I had to endure.

I am a North Korean escapee. After crossing the

border at the age of 18, I was lost in China and Mongolia for two years before I finally reached South Korea in 2006. My father, who owned a business in the Najin province, told me to cross the border unless I wanted to starve to death with the rest of the family. It has been more than ten years since I've left home.

Because I came to the South alone, there were no family members that could come to my graduation. Instead, many friends came to support me because they knew how much effort it took for me to graduate. Looking at their smiling faces, I felt that the past six years of hard work was well worth it.

Adapting to the South Korean society felt harder than crossing the border. An escapee has to use the energy a normal person can use for a lifetime to cross the border. Once you cross however, the harsh realities of society hit you hard without waiting for you to catch your breath. It is easy to lose the sense of yourself once you experience the towering walls of society. And although it has already been 8 years since I have come to South Korea, I still struggle to completely adapt to their standards. Every day, I discover a new side of me as I turn myself into the shape the society wants me to be.

The One with Strawberry Syrup and Americano

I had no intentions of going to university when I first came to the South. I didn't know anything about this place. Shortly after I arrived, I started working at a donut shop. One day, a customer asked for an Americano with syrup in it. I had never drunk an Americano before, but I made it the way I was trained to. The real problem was: what is a "syrup"? I opened the cupboard to find this "syrup" the customer was talking about. I finally found one that had the label on it and poured it in the coffee. After a sip, the customer called on the manager, angry with the weird strawberry flavored Americano. It turned out that I put in the strawberry syrup that they used for smoothies instead of sugar syrup.

After making mistakes like that for three days in a row, the boss handed me a hundred bucks and told me he had to let me go. That's when I realized that I was practically worthless in this country. Although South Korea was a prosperous country, it did not change the fact that I was only a North Korean escapee with nothing to offer. But I didn't want to live as a "nobody" forever. I needed to learn to survive— and that's when I decided that I needed to go to college.

The One Where I Don't Understand the Jokes

It's still a mystery to me how I got accepted to Yenisei. When I read the college essay I wrote back then, I can't even understand what I was trying to say. Yonsei is a top ranked university that South Korean students work their butts off to get into. The only reason I got in was because I was North Korean.

Getting to study in Yonsei was definitely a privilege, but facing its rigor and surviving till graduation was completely my doing.

Competition was cutthroat. It seemed impossible to pace myself in such a race. On the first day of college, I couldn't even understand 10 percent of what my professor was saying— I couldn't even laugh at his jokes. As a person used to rigid rules and structures, the freedom that college life offered felt like violence to me. When the first day was over and I left the campus, I felt that I didn't belong there.

My first semester was a complete failure. I couldn't understand any of the lectures and I couldn't make friends as I crept deeper into loneliness and inferiority. Busy with school work, I did not have time to work and my debts slowly increased. Some days, I couldn't attend school because I didn't have the bus fare. At the end, I got a warning from school. When you receive a warning, you can't receive any scholarships, so I had to take a semester off to work for my tuition money.

I did a lot of soul searching during the semester I took off. I gradually realized that the reason for my big failure was because of my lack of confidence. I was embarrassed at the fact that I was from North Korea. I was worried that people would look at me weird for my unusual accent and was also annoyed when they asked me questions about North Korea.

That's when I started my "Becoming South Korean" project. Every night, I would read newspaper columns with a pen in my mouth to lose my North Korean accent. I copied words off of books to understand how South Koreans write. I read popular novels and Japanese comic books to blend in and make friends. I played the games they liked and listened to the music they enjoyed. I stopped contacting the fellow North Korean escapees I used to know. I felt that they could not help me become a part of this society.

For a year and a half I prepared. I cut my spending and saved everything I could. By the fall semester of 2010, I was able to pay my tuition and start school again. Because my Northern accent had faded, less people asked me where I was from. My confidence grew and I started to make friends. Everything they knew of as common sense to me was a reality I had to learn. Whenever I met my South Korean friends I was so nervous that my back was drenched in sweat by the time our conversations ended. Every day I changed the masks I wore and lived the life of someone else.

Although I didn't hide the fact that I was from North Korea, I did my best to make my friends feel that I was a part of them. These friends helped me with my studies and by the end of the semester, I received the GPA score of 3.3 out of 4.3. I had achieved my dreams of getting over a 3.0.

The real problem came when I had to face myself. Outside, I did my best to forget my North Korean self and pretended to be from the South, but as soon as I went back home, I met my real North Korean self and felt lonely. My body that had been tense all day would all of a sudden relax and I wouldn't have the energy to do anything else. Once I came in, I did not want to head outside again and I wondered if it was wise to inflict such pain on myself.

The One With the Professor

I had to hide myself like a fugitive although it's not a sin to be born in North Korea. I asked myself the reason I hid countless times but could not reach an answer. As the semesters progressed and nothing changed, I fell into depression and I felt like I couldn't bear it any longer.

I had come to this college to get a degree— my only objective was to graduate. In Yonsei University, there is a subject called "chapple" that all students have as a graduation requirement. Chapple classes are normally taken by freshman or sophomore students, but I was unaware of that and had to take it in my junior year. To take the class as a junior I needed a signature from a professor and I had to go and see him. I was blankly looking around the room when he saw me.

"Who are you?"

"My name's Kim Hye"

"And who's that?"

"I'm a history major here and I needed your signature for the chapple classes."

The professor of small disposition looked at me sharply over his thick glasses.

"Do you not even know how to introduce yourself properly? You should have presented clearly your grade and major the moment you saw me."

After the reproach, I nervously redid my "improper" self-introduction. A few days later, the professor called me into his room. He handed me a white envelope. Inside, there were twelve 100 dollar bills.

"Some of the professors and I sometimes gather our own money to help out students that need aid, but we didn't know about you until recently", he said apologetically. "There's not much in there but we hope it helps."

He smiled gently. Although the society seems cold and unforgiving at times, there are some good people even in this country. The warmth of the professor's hands remained on the envelope for a long while.

The One Where It Takes a Day to Read a Page

As I became a junior and studies for my declared major officially started, school work became even harder. The academic works used words that made me feel like I was reading Korean as a foreign language. One time when I was reading a book on Orientalism, I translated the book's Korean into the Korean I knew and spoke. I didn't understand why people explained the most simple concepts with such complicated terms. I was even led to think that books were written in this way just so the academia community can exclude people like me.

It took a very long time to finish a book. I used to read a single page of a college thesis for 10 times just to understand what it was about. Being a history major, I had to write many reports and essays, but I didn't know where to start. Days passed of me sitting in my lectures, not understanding a word the professor was saying.

I had the fear of repeating what happened in the first semester of freshman year so I promised myself one thing: just aim to understand one thing for every lecture. To pay attention during lectures, I fixated my eyes on the professor's face and movements. I ferociously looked into his eyes as I took as much notes as I can.

English was my worst subject. This must be what many North Korean university students agree on. I joined the club Yonsei Global(YG) where it would pair me with a foreign exchange student. I met many foreigners through this club. As I met them more frequently, I experienced how my English abilities became better at an unbelievably fast pace. I even invited some of them to my house and serve dinner. To my foreigner friends, I was not a North Korean but an Asian.

After three years of extreme pressure, I dared to dream of happiness. Although it was necessary to be strict on yourself to grow and survive in a capitalist society, it felt wrong to inflict such pain on myself to the level of suffocation. With the money I made with my part time job during the semester, I went traveling that summer vacation. The friends I made through YG program helped me with free accommodation and food overseas.

In the summer of 2013, I visited my friend's house in Corsica, France. Corsica was a small village in the countryside of Southern France. I remember an old lady I met there. She held my hands tight when she heard that I was from North Korea.

"My son is in Brazil as an exchange student. I always feel worried about my son and miss him so much, but

I can still fly to him anytime I want. Now imagine what your mother feels. She can't see the young daughter she has sent away."

She embraced me and cried and cried. I had buried my memories of North Korea deep in my heart to only show my bright side to people in South Korea. I dared not even think of the word "mother" in fear of my throbbing heart. I simply couldn't afford dwelling on the past.

The way the old French lady of different race and nationality cried for me and worried about my mother made me feel like a family from this faraway land.

Through my travels I learned the confidence I needed to live in South Korea as a North Korean. Whether it is a wealthy country or one in need of desperate help, there were still the people and they weren't that different from me.

As I continued my time in university I learned the

same thing: that South Koreans too, were human beings. My South Korean friends sincerely helped me so I can catch up in school. I gave up on competing with them. All of them were my mentors. I would carefully watch their every move and tried to learn from them. I would borrow their essays to analyze and trace their words. I worked as hard as them and my grades improved steadily. Professors encouraged me as they proudly saw my progress as I developed one step at a time.

The One Where My North Korean Friends Leave Korea

I was glad to finally return the help I had only received until then. I was no longer the "North Korean friend", but just "a friend". Because I was older and had more experience, my South Korean friends often confessed on their worries and insecurities to me. We talked about a wide array of things— love, future, the society. The journey we went through to become true friends is what I believe true unification will be like.

Through my South Korean friends' help, I soon had the stability of the mind and heart to listen to other's problems. I started attending North Korean escapee meetings and made friends. I was no longer lonely. Once I graduated from a South Korean university, I lived with the confidence that I could do anything.

Many of my North Korean friends struggled life in college and left Korea. They spread out into various countries like England, Canada, and Belgium. My escapee friends couldn't endure the societal discrimination they had to face in the South. They thought that if they were going to be discriminated in a small world anyways, they would prefer facing racial discrimination in a bigger world.

My life in South Korea was also arduous. Although many people offered me the chance to go to another country, I could not leave, not because of the language barrier or anything else, but the fact that South Korea had given me an opportunity I could not give up on. The Korean society had offered many opportunities and I did not want my hard work to become in vain. Also, there was no guarantee that my situation in a foreign country would be better than that in Korea. I was prepared to overcome the walls that were presented to me by this society.

Now I am no longer a college student. There are no friends, professors, and my school to come to my aid now, and I have to withstand everything on my own. For 8 months, I worked hard to get a job before graduation. I sent letters to all the companies I could think of. But I did not get a single opportunity to even have an interview.

I almost fell into devastation again. Did I not have anything that I can offer to this society? For all the support I received in college, it was now my turn to play a role in society, and that is the reason why I continue to look for a job.

In many cases, people from North Korea have little to no opportunity of getting a job in the South even if the escapee has a bachelor's degree. Perceptions of them at work are not good since so many give up halfway through their career. But I will try and challenge myself. As I know the importance of a job, I will work hard until the end to become a rightful member of the South Korean society. I want to return the help that I've received while I climbed up the gates of a college education.

According to an educational institution of North Korean escapees, only 1 out of 10 escapees that enter universities is able to get a college degree. Those that give up in the middle work at minimum wage jobs and make their ends meet as the low income class of society or emigrate to countries like Norway or Canada as refugees from a third world country.
The Shin Donga Newspaper, 04/2014

WAIT FOR ME

Prologue

Time never rests; it endlessly flows. Even at this age, I feel like I would someday return to the home I used to have. I can't shake away the feeling that I left home the day before yesterday. Don't get me wrong— I have walked a long and wary path that seemed to have no end, and I have grown old over the years. Back then I was in my 20s, and how old am I now?

A few years ago, I wrote these accounts to remember everything that had happened. How foolish I was to be scared of my forgetfulness, because memory is a funny thing. Every day, the recollections of the past become clearer and clearer and my nightmares visit me to haunt me with images and emotions, more alive than ever.

It was a time of unreal reality as the tides crashed against my lone body.

I. Where I was Born

I was born neither in the countryside nor the city. The village I was born in was a farmland but also close to the city. It was a cozy place.

The mountain's streams flowed in front of our house. In springtime, a wild arrangement of rhododendrons and magnolias would bloom into a euphoria of colors. In fall, there would be a white, mist-like smoke that clouded the window, and we would dry herbs and vegetables on a big flat rock in front of our home. My father was born there, and so were his children. My withered sister probably still lives there.

It is commonly acknowledged in North Korea that the parent's job usually determines their children's profession.

My parents were intelligent and wise. My mother, who used to live in China, learned how to become a teacher like grandfather. After she graduated college, she came to North Korea with my father. On the other hand, my father was so poor that he couldn't go to college and studied medicine alone. He treated patients in our own house, including us three sisters.

Because my parents weren't born into a honorable family, they had no other choice but to do hard labor to make ends meet. Growing up, I never saw my grandfather and soon learned that our family was not of "good roots". We didn't have a single picture of my father's family, and our parents would never talk about his family. Not that us sisters were curious about them, that is.

II. Childhood

I remember my mother being sick ever since I was in kindergarten. By the time I was an *Inmin* school student, she would frequently be bedridden in hospital. But things improved as I became a middle school student. Mother left the hospital and would only visit there every once in a while. Remembering this makes me think of the *gangnengyi* noodles and rice I used to make when I was seven. Here in South Korea, whenever I see how seven year olds are treated as the children they are, it reminds me that this is a good place to live in.

My first attempts to make noodle were disasters; when the water started boiling, I was too scared to take out the noodles from the burning hell of the pot. After moments of hesitation, the noodles soon turned into soup. I was scared of my mother's reproach, but surprisingly, she smiled graciously and consoled me with compliments. Gently, she taught me how to use a *chae* to take out the noodles from the boiling water. There was another time when I dropped my rice washing bowl while cooking dinner. I deftly went down on my knees to scrape the rice from the ground but it was too late. The rice wasn't washed well and was burnt.

As the first child, I considered it common sense to take responsibility to fill in mother's position in the family. When I returned home, I would cook rice instead of doing homework and at dinner I would prepare *gangnengyi* rice for the next morning. Deep into the night, I would iron my little sister's school uniform for the next school day.

To this day, I sometimes sadly ask myself why I didn't live for myself in those years.

III. Like the Others

Like other families, our family had less to eat starting in the 90s. The Farm distributed months' worth of rice, but my mother's family raided our house on a regular basis, constantly asking for food. My mother was the youngest of six brothers and sisters.

When grandfather and grandmother died, my two aunts lived in our house as if it was their own. This led to fights between mother and father— it's hard to be understanding and patient when people are hungry. Father had three children to look after and the situation in our village was not good. Ever since the 90s started, it was everybody's job to wake up in the morning to check if their neighbors had passed the night safely. The situation was *that* bad.

Our house was not an exception. One day when I returned from work, everybody at home seemed intense and angry. My uncle had come to ask for some pine tree powder that my father had rummaged to find in the mountains. His young son dangled from his back.

"Our family really needs to get our shit together!" mother cried.

She couldn't afford to think of her siblings when her own family barely stayed afloat. Upset from the unexpected reproach, my uncle stayed only a single night and left.

Mother was angry. But I was angrier.

I had taken responsibilities of the mother figure in the family for a long time. Whenever anyone came to ask for charity, I made sure that they knew they were not welcome in our house. There was simply not enough for everyone to eat.

In North Korea, unless you are born in an honorable family, it is almost impossible to be successful unless you prove yourself worthy in a university or the military. The same rule applied to our family. What success or personal dream could I hope to achieve in this society when my parents were mere laborers? The one thing that brightened up the household was that my two younger sisters excelled at school. My mother even managed to become the president of the parent's association until middle school.

With their academic talent and my mother's support, my first sister was accepted to one of the few universities in the region and the younger one passed the exam for the School of Medicine. It was only on her first day of school, however, that she realized that her spot had been stolen by another girl.

Surprised, my mother and sister went to the university to check her exam results again. In turned out that a daughter of a professor in the university had taken my sister's spot. The daughter was enrolled under my sister's name. We felt a sense of defeat— but what could we do? Our family was not from good roots and we did not know anyone in power. Thankfully, my sister studied hard for another year and got accepted to the college my first sister went to.

There was nothing left of our laborer family when my parents sent my two sisters to college. A few months later when my second sister returned home, she was in a ghastly condition and seemed to suffer from a disease. Her face was hollow and she had no strength in her body. My mom held her tight and we all cried for a while. Our family didn't have money to send her. We could barely find anything to feed our own mouths. My sister told us how the university cafeteria didn't have rice and gave out meals once in every few days. Students like my sister who had no financial support from home had no other option but to starve.

My mother's family continued to come raid our family in the middle of this chaos. My father was angry and my mother was agitated. I felt that if things continued this way, something bad was going to happen, so ignoring what was demanded of me as a member of the Communist Party and a laborer in the fields, I started working in the market. My name was soon on the Party's black list. Now that I think of it, I don't understand how I had the courage to go to the marketplace every day. Hunger made me blind to fear.

IV. My Niece

Years passed and I became a mature woman. By then, my second sister finished university and was commissioned to a labor group (the "third revolution group") close to our hometown, so she returned home to live with us.

Around that time, most of the village boys that had left for the military were returning home as well. Marriage proposals flooded, especially now that my sister returned. The little boys and girls who used to be childhood friends, entirely uninterested in each other, became shy men and women.

My sister had a sweet face and was the only girl in our region that had a college degree. Many eyes were on her as boys suspiciously wondered around our house too often. Most of them were a year older than me (except for two boys, all of the boys in the upper class man had joined the military after high school). It amazed me how every single one of them had returned home.

In North Korea, men and women, even in their prime stage of youth, don't talk to each other much. So imagine how shy everyone was after a long time of not seeing each other.

Although I was very strong and masculine, I was shy and introverted in the inside. Unless a man directly asked me a question, I wouldn't even look at him in the eye. My sister was different. Everything from her looks to her personality was brighter, more cheerful. More and more men sought her out, and one day, my sister told my mother that Lee had asked her for marriage. Lee was one of the upperclassman boys that had returned from Pyongyang after serving as a bodyguard for the military. Their family's "roots" were far more superior to ours. His father was actually the Secretary of my labor group. I hated his father and often cursed him. How funny it was, that his son was courting my little sister. Lee followed around my sister like a puppy and it became hard for me to hate his father.

I tried to scoff at their relationship. Having a man wasn't the most important thing in life. But as the two's courtship became deeper, my father increasingly yelled at me for not finding a partner of my own. He would yell stuff at me to a point where I wondered whether he was really my biological father. Mother also constantly reminded me that I should soon get a man considering my age.

Soon enough, I was introduced to a man who lived in the city by my uncle. I only considered "roots" when I chose my partner. His wealth and abilities weren't even a factor. Everybody was starving anyways.

While my relationship with the man slowly progressed, my sister continued to meet her suitor. Whenever I wasn't around, the boy would come visit her in our house and persuade father and mother. My sister seemed to like him as well. From morning to night, he would hang around my sister when he didn't have work. They got married that summer and a year later, I had a cute niece.

V. I Get Hurt

I used to consider myself very mature. Years of looking after my sisters and doing the housework made me feel like a grown up, but these days as I remember how mean and authoritative I was to my sisters, my heart fills with regret and humility. I wish I had smiled more and listened to what they had to say.

My ugly temper reached its height on my sister's wedding day. Busy with studies and work, my sister forgot to clean her underwear for her wedding day, so she asked me for a pair of my new ones. Instead of offering mine before she asked me, I refused to give mine to her. I swore and yelled at my sister for asking me for such things. I swore so loud that my father came out of his room to ask me what the problem was. On the day that should have been the happiest day of her life, my sister broke into tears— all because of a single sheet of underwear I wouldn't lend. I didn't deserve to be the smiling sister standing next to my younger sister in the wedding photo. My heart aches even in this moment as I write this down.

As soon as my sister's wedding was over, I was once again out on the streets to make money. By then, I started working as a train vendor.

The train never came on time. That one day, it was no different. As I waited for the train in the station with a big bag full of merchandise, the train finally rolled in. Unlike the other days, it was an express train.

Paying no attention, I quickly got on the train. People that had been waiting in the station for days shoved themselves in against the meager attempts of the workers to maintain order. Because my bag was too heavy, I couldn't board the train. I sat on the steps of the train. As soon as I sat down, the train rumbled and started to chug along.

The express train was fast. As I pressed my face against my bags to avoid the cold wind, something sharp hit me in the ribs. I led out a strange animal noise because of the pain. It felt like somebody was cutting apart the veins in my heart. Instantly, I felt my body losing control of itself. Even in that painful moment, I still managed to look out, searching for what had hit me. There was nothing but the fields as the train chugged along. Later on as I think of it, I think it was a rock that bounced off the train wheels that hit my ribs.

My arms were losing control as my grip became weaker every second. I held on to the staircase with all my might with the thought that if I let go, I would be trampled by the train wheels. I unconsciously felt my legs being dragged along the rails. After minutes of fierce fighting, the train arrived at the next station. Barely able to open my eyes, I grabbed onto the train. I heard the faint sound of the train's screams. Trying to stand up, I lost my consciousness in the station.

When I woke up, I was in the hospital.

VI. His Death

When I regained my consciousness, I asked the patient sitting next to me why I was there. The patient told me that people transported me there from the station when I blacked out. A nurse walked in and asked me my address. I was afraid to tell her. The thought of being a burden to my family made me contemplate. I was not only injured but also extremely malnourished. My family barely had enough to eat themselves and had no money. If my nurse gave them a call, they would scrape the last bit of money and food they had to come to the hospital. I couldn't allow that to happen.

The hospital was impatient for me to leave as I wasn't able to afford my own medicine. They told me that another blow would kill me and that they didn't have any medicine left for me. I gave my last bag of rations (the one I was going to sell) to the nurse and in return received antibiotics for another two days. Blood transfusion was out of the question and I had to leave the hospital. My toes had a reddish black color from being dragged along the railroad tracks.

Although I had survived, the journey back home was too much for me. I stopped by my uncle's house to rest for a few days. His house didn't have a single bowl of porridge so I had to lie in bed like a corpse.

I finally got home after fifteen days of rest. Cholera was spreading throughout the country back then, and I later on learned that my mother had been worried that I had not returned for so long because of the disease. When I stepped into my house, mother didn't recognize who I was.

My mother and sister cried as they clung on to me, asking where I had been and telling me that father had been asking for me. Without a moment to explain where I had been, I anxiously asked where father was. My pregnant sister started to tell me how our aunt visited our house without knowing that she had cholera. At first, everyone thought they had the cold because the symptoms were not obvious. My mother, who had always been the weakest in the family, was the first to fall sick. Soon, the whole family broke down, and surprisingly, it was father who had taken the fatal blow. If you failed to fight back the disease for three days, it took you away.

My family had been in the midst of their own turmoil while I was gone. The hospital didn't have medicine for my sister and the baby she had inside of her. They told her that it would be hard for the child and mother to both live, but she fought back ferociously, and it was unexpectedly our father who had died.

I resented my aunt for bringing death upon us. Ever since he married mother, father had spent all his life in supporting our family as well as our aunts and uncles. He nursed the failing health of my mother and was always by her side. Everybody believed that she would be the first to go.

The moment my father got the epidemic, he lost strength. When my sister took him to the hospital, they said it was too late. He returned home after two days and passed away the next day. The day before he died, he told mother that he was worried that I had not returned and that he wanted to eat *gangnengyi* rice with *ssam*. We didn't have rice, and cholera made everything he ate come back out again. Mother got milk from the two goats we had and mixed it with potatoes to give to my failing father. On his last night, they say he asked for me, murmured the *gangnengyi* he wanted to eat, and reminded mother that they should plant beans for next year so they could make *tojang*. At dawn, he left.

My father had wanted to live somewhere quiet, so we had moved near the mountain where there wasn't electricity. The village was so far away from our house that it was hard to tell people of his death. The one neighbor we had locked their doors and shut their windows when my sister yelled at them that father had died. Later on, they told us that they had no other choice because they had lost two of their children from an epidemic a few years ago. My mother and sister had to struggle up the mountain all alone with my father's coffin. Few people made it to the funeral.

VII. *Chuseok*

Time didn't stop for my father's death. While the sun and moon rise by nature's law and people change through the flow of time, the only thing that doesn't change is time itself. Not long after my father died, the national holiday *Chuseok* came.

Back in the old days, sons were valued very much in families. I still remember hearing my father coming back from work, angry that the other laborers looked down on him for not having a son. Even after our father's death, however, his helpless daughters were no help. We could do nothing but weep.

I hadn't visited his grave since I returned home. It was only when *Chuseok* ran around that I had the chance to visit him. I piggyback rode my beloved niece and walked up the mountain. The mountain was bare and did not have grass. The clay was red and his shabby gravestone was carelessly thrusted into the ground. Tears welled up and the emotions that had been suppressed streamed down my face. My sister was in a fit as she wailed hysterically.

"Father, father, the grandson you wanted so bad is finally here…" my sister cried.

I couldn't understand myself at that moment. Father had been equally kind to all three of his daughters— so why couldn't I cry as much as my sister?

Although I cried less, my heart still grieved for him. I couldn't help but feel that father would rise and come to me if I just called his name. That was the last time I ever saw his grave.

Once I reached my new home, I was able to hear about the news of father's grave from my sisters. They said after I left home, his stone was made again and grass grew on the mountains to cover the red soil. To this day, however, all I can picture is the lonely red mountain where my father's gravestone once stood.

After *Chuseok,* word that the government would distribute meager amounts of food made me work in the market again. It was only after I heard that my uncle crossed the river that I changed my mind.

VIII. The Start of the Cross

Success in the marketplace did not depend on hard work but luck. If I was lucky, I would get 2kg worth of rice. If not, I would get less than a kilogram. But however it was, my work prevented my family's starvation. The work was hard but I had to keep on going to keep my family stay afloat. At times when my body reached its limits, I wondered if there would be a day in my life when I wouldn't have to go to the market.

Then one day, something unexpected was waiting for me at home. My youngest uncle had crossed the river from China and was back in our house. As I mentioned earlier, my mother grew up in China, and while her father lived in North Korea, my mother's cousins all remained in China. My uncle had crossed the river to go visit them. Although I've heard stories about crossing the river before, I never imagined that anybody in my family would attempt such a thing.

As soon as I heard of this, I was mad at my uncle. He had always come to our house to ask for help and food. Why didn't he bring me along instead of his friends to China? All he had brought back for us from China was candy. If my uncles and aunts hadn't raided our family so often, I wouldn't have had to start working from such an early age. Maybe my father wouldn't have died either. I was mad. That's when I decided to cross the river myself.

Uncle told me that he made a promise with his Chinese cousins to meet by the docks on a set date. If they didn't appear in the docks, my uncle would cross the river again. My mother was delighted at the thought of seeing her cousins again. She also worried their safety on crossing the river. I decided that if my cousins didn't show up, I would cross the river myself. More than the reunion of our family, I was excited about the food and things they would bring over from China.

The day finally arrived and our entire family went to the docks. We waited and waited. Our eyes hurt from staring out into the river. Our stomachs, as always, started to growl. Waiting had its limits. I turned to mother and told her my plan. She stared at me, struck with worry. Horror stories of what they did to people who were caught during an attempt to cross made her anxious. But knowing my temper, she knew she couldn't stop me. She knew that if I had my heart set onto something, nothing could stop me. My uncle was initially against the idea as well, but after much persuading, he agreed that I was to cross with him and his friend. For a week, we planned the crossing. Mother told me if she didn't hear from me for three days, she would return home knowing that I crossed the river safely.

The day finally came. We decided to cross the river under the Onsung International Train bridge where my uncle had crossed for the first time. We ate dinner and drank. Mother told my uncle's friend that too much drinking wouldn't be good when we were crossing. The man told us that the alcohol would help him with his anxiety and that we needed to drink to cross without fear. Since it was considered disrespectful for a woman to talk back to an adult, I stayed quiet.

During the days we spent preparing for the crossing, I noticed that my uncle's friend talked a lot, especially when he was drunk. I was worried that the man was drinking too much on such an important day. But I couldn't take away his wretched bottle from him.

The width of the river was wide. But it was not only the river but the distance to the riverbank that was the problem. It was winter and the lake was frozen, so we only had to get to the riverbank safely.

After dinner, we briefly exchanged looks and started on our way. The moonlight was bright and I could see the others clearly. We got to the riverbank safely, but the drunk man couldn't seem to shut up. Maybe he was scared, or simply too drunk, but every time he stepped on a rock, he would mutter "everything is alright" to himself. The night was quiet and there was not a single sound from the winds. Every breath was audible.

Just when we had 3 steps left to the riverbank, somebody yelled, "Hands up!". We all froze and rose our hands. Six guards surrounded us with guns pointed at us.

IX. The State Security Department

A soldier had heard one of the drunk man's mutters. I could not believe it. A bottle of alcohol had ruined our entire plan. The guards guffawed and said they caught yet another married couple. The drunk man and I meekly told them we weren't married. Oftentimes, soldiers caught married couples in their attempts to cross the river.

The soldiers searched our coats and pockets. They seemed disappointed that we didn't hold any tobacco or money for them to take. I realized with regret that we may have been let go if we had some money to give them. Once they knew we had no possessions, they tied our hands in ropes and started off for the State Security Department. As I walked, I just hoped that the drunk man would remember the backup story we came up with just in case we were caught. We had agreed on the story that I persuaded the man into crossing the river with me and that once we returned from China, I would pay him for accompanying me. Mother even wrote a small letter that stated how my cousins in China would help me protect the values of our Communist Party or something of that sort. That ridiculous piece of letter was what later on saved my life.

After walking for a long while, we passed the metal gates into a building where we were told to wait. The clock read 10 o'clock. We were taken into separate rooms to be interrogated. In a tiny dark room, an officer was waiting for me. The room was warm, and I was overwhelmed with fatigue. It all felt like a dream.

After a long interrogation, I got some sleep and was taken to another department. I believe it was a department that was one step higher than the place I was the day before. There were many military camps set around the building, and instead of being taken to the interrogation room, we were locked in the pantry for a while. It was cold and they didn't give us food. Some soldiers would come inside the pantry once in a while to pat on the man's trousers. It was no use— they couldn't find anything to steal. Because I was a woman, they didn't lay their hands on me. The last soldier that searched us seemed unsatisfied. He told my uncle's friend to take off his belt. We were surprised. How was the man supposed to wear his pants when all that was left of him were bones? He refused to give away his belt. The soldier cursed us that we would never be able to cross the river. He left. I felt bitter disappointment for my country— if we just had some money to pay the soldiers, we would have been freed to go.

It became the fourth day since we had eaten anything. We were transferred to yet another Department. As we walked to another building, the sunshine relieved me of the hunger and cold. The soldiers that surrounded us had guns with them. Our hands were tied with ropes. Next to the road, the dark Tumen River wildly flowed. All the ice had melted by the sunshine. The rapids seemed strong and the width was narrow. I wondered if the river was deep. One soldier laughed and told us that we should try crossing the river now. We laughed together at his jokes. Our walk to the Security Department was surprisingly calm and pleasant; we joked with the soldier and tried to focus on the sunlight.

Suddenly, a car appeared. When the soldier raised his hand, the car halted and we were ordered to get in. In the blink of an eye, we reached the iron gates of the State Security Department. All the hair on my body stood.

As we stepped in, guards instantly replaced our ropes with shackles. We had arrived at the notorious State Security Department. Every step I took and every rustle of the glinting grey shackles made my heart beat wild. When we passed the iron bars, there was a small hallway with many rooms.

The moment we stepped into one of the rooms, a fist flew into the face of my uncle's friend. Unable to protect himself from the unexpected blow, the man was left speechless. Another blow. And then another. But what could the poor man do? If a guard from the Security Department hits you, you have no other choice but to accept the beating. All the blood in my veins felt like it stopped. I had never seen a human being beaten like a beast. I had seen torture in the movies before, but I was unprepared to see it in real life. Humans were such fragile beings that could easily be beaten to death. At that moment, I sighed in relief that I was a woman.

The fact that my uncle's friend was a member of the Communist Party seemed to anger the guard further.

"You're a member of the Party?" he said.

"Yes— I am." croaked the poor man getting hit.

"Hey this son of a bitch says he's a member— what Party are you a part of?"

"The Military Party, sir."

"All you bastards in the Military Party are worthless—" the guard continued to kick the man's stomach.

My uncle's friend couldn't do anything but shriek and grunt like an animal. The guard continued to strike his empty stomach that had starved for four straight days. I thought he was going to die. I didn't dare breathe. The guard stopped kicking as he seemed to regain sanity. All the guards left us in the room. We later on learned that it was the room where newcomers to the Department were investigated. Other than myself and the my uncle's friend, there was a women and a man in the room.

I frantically told my uncle's friend that we have to stick to the story we came up with. Mistakes may end everything, I said. When the guard returned, the other man in the room told the guard that we planned a back-up story. That moment, I realized that the other man was no newcomer; he had already been a convict there for a while. He was barefoot and wore prison clothes. The woman next to him seemed young. She told me she already crossed the river numerous times. The array of plates and cloth that laid on the table were hers; she was bringing them back from China to make a living. The guard opened a cupboard that was in the corner of the room and took out a little piece of rice ball rolled up in a plastic bag. He handed the rice ball to the convict that snitched on us. The moment I saw the rice ball, I wanted it so bad. The upper half of the cupboard was filled with rice. The lower half was made up of *banchan*. The food was undoubtedly made from the families of the inmates.

Our interrogation continued until night. The fact that it was our first attempt to cross the river and my mother's fake letter were immense help. Soon, the interrogator unshackled me, saying that we should never meet again. Sighing in relief, I told him he would never have to see me. It was only my uncle's friend and I that were released. The woman with the cloth was to become an inmate. The moment she was handed over to the jail guards, the woman broke into tears. My heart throbbed— she was so young and was taken a prisoner in the prime time of life.

We were released late at night. A week had passed since our attempt to cross the river. We were back out in the outside world. The moment I was free, the advice of the interrogator disappeared from my mind. I was determined more than ever that I would cross the river.

X. A Promise that I Did Not Keep

The way back to my mother's arms was long. The night was so dark that I could barely see where I was walking. I wanted to crawl to find anything on the ground that could fill my stomach. Finding a place to sleep was another problem. I did not know where I was, nor did I know anybody. My uncle's friend was having an even harder time. Most men get easily slumped after a few days of starving. The man who was with me had not eaten or slept for days and had received a beating in the Security Department.

Walking along the streets, we decided to visit all the houses that had lights on. Since I was a woman and had a less threatening presence, I went around the neighborhood, knocking on doors. Back in those days, our people didn't welcome strangers into houses easily— not because of the lack of rooms but the lack of food. After numerous attempts, one house finally let us in.

It was the house of a labor manager. A father and a daughter lived there, and the father told us that he can sleep in his daughter's room. He gave us leftover rice and told his daughter to buy tofu for us. After eating the rice and tofu, we fell asleep. We were so grateful that we couldn't even express our gratitude fully. They even gave us breakfast. I will never forget what they did for us.

The next day, we went to the station where my mother worked. We could catch up to her because the train thankfully had not arrived on time. She thought that I had successfully crossed the river as I hadn't returned home. She was surprised to see me. As soon as I told her what happened, she decided to take me to the market. I asked why we were going there. We were penniless.

Mother told me she didn't want cobwebs in her daughter's mouth. She took off her jacket and gave me corn rice cake. I devoured that thing in seconds. I do not know what I looked like at the time, but I probably must have looked frightening. Giving me all the rice cake she had, we boarded the train heading home together. I said my farewells to my uncle's friend. He was too frail to go home, he said. That was the last time I saw that man.

In the market, mother sold her jacket and my sister's military pants. Those pants were a gift from my sister's fiancé. He had prepared it from his military days for his future wife and gave it to my sister the day he proposed to her. In the North, both women and men wear military apparel often.

My pretty sister looked good even in those pants and all the town girls were jealous of her. When mother and I were leaving for the border, she had given her precious pants to us. And we had to sell it.

The pants weren't well compensated for as there were plenty of military clothes near the border. Even the used Chinese clothes were sold at a higher price than our pants. Watching my mother sell those pants broke my heart and I promised to myself that I would cross the river successfully to come back with a stunning pair of pants for my sweet sister.

Mother and I returned to our house. My two sisters were surprised to see me and asked us where we had been. Mother and I did not dare say a word. After a few days of my absence, the house looked even more impoverished without my earnings from the market.

I knew I had to cross that river. After resting at home for a week, I was back on my way to the Tumen river. Maybe my determination showed through my actions— my sisters seemed to understand what I was trying to do. But I had no other choice. I had promised myself to cross the river.

I had a weird forlorn feeling hours before I boarded the train that would take me close to the border. My second sister had returned home early that day, giving off a lousy excuse and avoiding the real reason. It was finally night— the train would arrive soon, and I had to go.

I couldn't find my sister in the house and was about to leave without getting to say goodbye. I saw her in front of our door with her daughter in her arms, crying. She knew that this was the last decision I was making for my family. Trying to act calm, I opened the door to leave. My sister could not stop crying. I hugged her tight. Wrapped in my arms, my sister told me to come back safely. That was the last hug I gave to my beloved little sister. I was always so proud of that little girl.

As I picked up the small parcel to leave the house, mother told me she would accompany me. She seemed relieved when I told her I was going to stop by aunt's house. I wanted mother to stay with me longer— even an hour would be good enough. I looked out into the horizon. The Tumen River was narrow and the wind was cold. There seemed to be less guards in that part of the river. Mother, worried that I would fail at my second attempt, told me that we had to find the best part of the river to cross. I spent three days preparing for the cross in my aunt's house.

Although I promised myself I wouldn't show weakness, I couldn't help it when mother was around. She had married father at an early age and raised me dearly. Her sickness made her depend on me every day, and I pitied that. She lost her husband too soon and was ill, yet she would never lay in bed for us sisters. I prayed that nothing happened to my family while I was away.

The day was short and it was already getting dark outside. I stood on the river bank with Mother. I tried not to cry, but the moment I saw Mother's face, I couldn't hold them back.

"I wish I don't have to let you go" she said.

She took off her jacket and gave it to me with towels. It was the nicest pair she had unlike the shabby clothes I brought from home. I knew that I would have to sell them anyways as soon as I got to China. I pleaded her to keep the towels and the jacket, reminding her that I would return in two months. Mother told me that it is dangerous to cross once the river melted and advised me to spend the summer in grandfather's house to return next winter. I refused to listen to her. I told her that she needed me and that I would return in two months no matter what happened.

Mother and I went inside a building by the river to see if there were any guards. When I saw that the coast was clear, I crossed the river without second thought. I succeeded in crossing the river. Looking out for the guards, I didn't even have the chance to look at Mother's face. In that moment, I had forgotten entirely about her.

As I regained calmness after crossing the river, I searched frantically for Mother. I only managed to see a small figure across the river, running up a hill. Mother told me earlier that day that she would try to see me as long as possible. Noticing that I had left the building, she had already run up the hill to see if I crossed safely. Barely able to see her figure, I couldn't stop the tears spilling out of my eyes. Covering my mouth with hands, I wept silently. This was how I parted with my mother and sister. The two months I had promised became well over two years. My promise was not kept.

Whenever I remember my last moment with Mother and her eyes, full of tears and worry, I cannot stop my own tears from falling. I later on learned from a phone call that she had waited for my return until the end. She never forgot my promise. Unable to tell anybody of her worries, she had to deal with her aching heart alone. She went to the river bank where we parted for countless times. I can clearly picture my mother, missing and worrying for me until the day of her death. At times I feel like I can hear her voice. The guilt that I could not keep my promise and my helplessness in being by her side in her last moments weigh down on me every day.